jigsaw

Bible discovery for young children

Edited by Christine Wright

SCRIPTURE UNION

ISBN 1 85999 090 8

British Cataloguing-in-Publication Data.

A catalogue record for this book is available from the British Library

Acknowledgements

Writers:
Elizabeth Alty
Margaret Barfield
Liz Lunn
Christine Orme
Margaret Spivey

Artists:
Sonia Canals
Sue Cony
Eira Reeves
Angie Sage

Design:
Mark Carpenter Design Consultants

Published in the UK by Scripture Union,
207 – 209 Queensway, Bletchley,
Milton Keynes MK2 2EB

Distributed in Australia by Scripture Union,
PO Box 2915, Fitzroy DC Victoria 3065

Distributed in South Africa by SUPA
83 Campground Road Rondebosch 7700

Distributed in New Zealand by Scripture
Union, 9A Oxford Terrace, PO Box 760,
Newtown, Wellington

Distributed in Singapore by Scripture Union,
7 Armenian Street, 03 – 07 Bible House,
Singapore 0617

Distributed in Malaysia by Scripture Union,
Bangunan SU, 386 Jalan 5/59, 46000
Petaling Jaya, Selangor

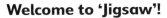

Welcome to 'Jigsaw'!

The aim of this book (and of the others in the series) is to help you explore the Bible with your family.

When children are small, before they can read, it can be hard to know how to introduce the Bible to them. 'Jigsaw' offers a very simple way which is enjoyable as well.

When you read the Bible, you notice that ideas about God are often put over through stories or pictures that help us understand better. We read about water, growing, building, wood and meals, for instance.

There are eight topics in this book. Each topic in this book encourages investigation around one of these pictures. This is presented in three ways.

The topics begin with two pages of introductory activities. Use them to remind each other of feelings, thoughts and memories about the topic – things you know already.

Bible stories

Enjoy the stories together. You may want to read them more than once and to do any actions or discuss the pictures.

Choose the ideas that suit your family. Some of these will help everyone learn more about the topic. Some suggest prayers or other ways of thinking about God. Some are just for fun. All of them will remind you of the Bible stories.

There is no 'right' way to use 'Jigsaw'! You can read it every day, dipping into a topic for several days running. If you do this, read the stories several times and try a different activity each day – or repeat one which you've enjoyed already.

Or use 'Jigsaw' less frequently and spend longer looking at a topic together, trying out several activities.

Or you might like to dip into several topics one after the other, then come back to do more from each one when you like.

It's really up to you! But children do enjoy hearing stories again and again and they like doing activities more than once. So don't feel that you can only do things once.

It is hoped that through using 'Jigsaw' your child will learn to associate the Bible with pleasure and with warm feelings. You'll be surprised how much you all learn about God too!

Contents

Hello! My name is Jig-sparrow! I hope you like this 'Jigsaw' book. There are lots of things in it for you to do and there are stories to share with your family.

Look out for me on the pages of the book. You'll see me on the Bible story pages.

Do you have a Bible at home? If you do, look for it now and keep it with your 'Jigsaw' book. The Bible is full of stories and other interesting things. I'm here to help you and your family enjoy using the Bible together.

Have fun!

The wind

A windy day

Sean and Dad have gone
for a walk. How do you
know that it's a windy day?

Look and listen

I look through the window and what do I see?
The grass and the flowers are waving to me.
The wind's gently swaying the leaves of the tree
And butterflies are dancing along with the breeze.

Bustling and gusting and twisting around –
The wind's playing wild games all over the town.
It's catching the dry dust and tossing it round
And chasing the litter along on the ground.

The wind's sneaking in through the joins in
     my clothes.
It's making my ears ache and hurting my nose.
With sharp icy fingers, it's freezing my toes
And my knees and my chin and my cheeks,
     as it blows.

Nothing is stirring; the wind's gone away,
No huffing or puffing or bluster today;
No soft breath of fresh air to whisper and play,
Just quiet, and stillness, and calmness – all day.

The wind and the water

Exodus 14:21-31

God's special people, the Israelites, had waited for hundreds of years to get away from Egypt. At last King Rameses of Egypt had agreed to let them leave and they had started on their journey straight away.

They walked and walked till they were quite worn out. Then, they rested and camped for the night near the marshy lakes of the Sea of Reeds. Suddenly, the quiet of the camp was shattered by a shriek: 'Help! Soldiers!'

Everyone leapt up and stared in terror to see the mighty Egyptian army heading straight for them! King Rameses of Egypt had changed his mind. He was coming to get the Israelites back.

'Run!' someone suggested.

But where could they run to? There was sea on one side and the Egyptians on the other.

The people turned to Moses, their leader, and all started shouting.

'Moses! 'What are we going to do? We'll all be killed!'

'Don't be afraid,' soothed Moses. 'God's brought us this far. He will look after us and help us.'

Moses stood at the edge of the sea and held out his hand. A strong wind began to blow and blow. The people shivered but were too busy watching Moses to bother about the cold.

Something peculiar was happening to the sea. The wind was blowing the water away! A pathway had appeared through the middle of the sea all the way to the other shore. There was a wall of water on each side, but the gap in the middle was dry.

'Come along,' ordered Moses. 'Let's go through before the soldiers get us!'

The Israelites did not need to be told twice. They scurried and scuffled and stumbled across the seabed as fast as they could go.

As soon as they reached the other side, Moses held out his hand again. The wind stopped blowing and the steep walls of water collapsed and the path disappeared under a churning mass of sea.

'Hooray!' they all cheered. And the Israelites went on their way singing and dancing and thanking God.

What happened next?

Mark 6:45-51

1. Jesus had gone for a walk to talk to God alone. His friends were in their boat trying to row across the lake, but they were not getting very far.

Why was it so hard for them to row?

What happened next?

2. Jesus' friends saw him coming towards them. But they were in the middle of the lake, so how did he reach them?

What happened next?

3. The friends were all so scared to see Jesus walking on the water that they began to shout.

What do you think Jesus said to them?

What happened next?

4. Jesus said, 'Don't be afraid. It's me, Jesus.'

He got into the boat and the wind stopped blowing. The friends rowed across the lake

Music in the air

Make some wind chimes to hang indoors or out, where they will catch the breeze. You could use bamboo garden canes cut into different lengths or sea shells. A grown-up will have to drill holes, but you can help thread them on to strings so that the bamboo or sea shells touch each other when the wind blows. Hang the strings from a wire coat-hanger.

Outside in the wind

When you're outside, look out for what the wind is doing. Is it blowing hard or softly? Is it warm or cold? Can you see and hear leaves moving? Spot litter blowing along. Look at trees to see how their shape is changed by the wind. Find seeds scattered by the wind, like dandelions, sycamore keys. Blow a dandelion clock and pretend to tell the time. See how the wind ripples a puddle or a pond. Watch clouds moving across the sky.

Make your own windy day!

Fold a strip of paper, concertina style, and tape one end. Spread out the paper to make a fan and cool yourself and everyone else!

Windy day picture

Make your own windy day scene by pasting bits and pieces to a sheet of card. Try a sky scene (cotton wool clouds, kites, balloons, blown leaves etc); or a sea scene (boats, high waves, flags flying).

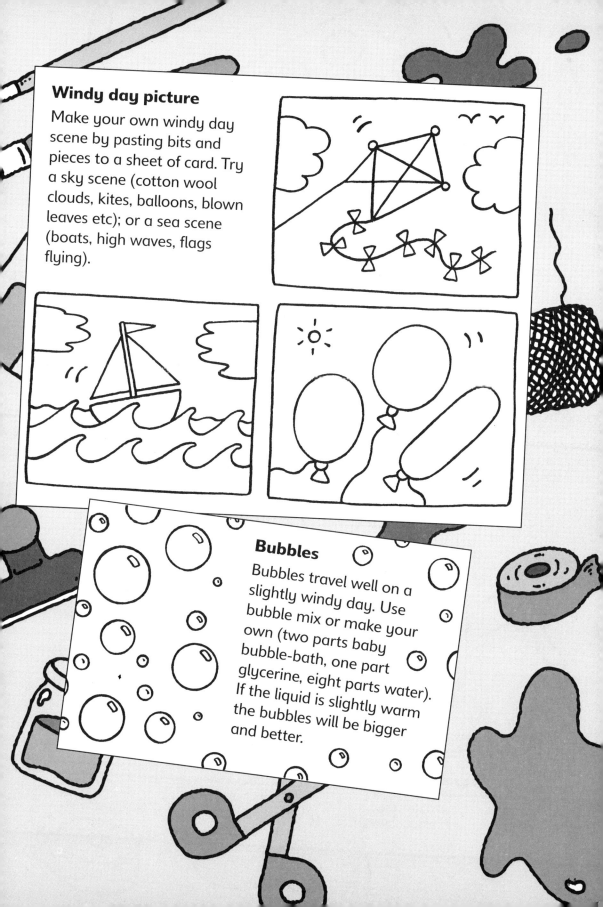

Bubbles

Bubbles travel well on a slightly windy day. Use bubble mix or make your own (two parts baby bubble-bath, one part glycerine, eight parts water). If the liquid is slightly warm the bubbles will be bigger and better.

God sends the wind

Based on Psalm 78:26

God sends the wind from west
and east,
From north and south through
all the land.
Wherever it blows,
Wherever it blows,
It comes and goes at
God's command.

Let's go fly a kite

Find a large strong paper bag and cut across the bottom. Punch holes for string in the top and tape around the holes. Tie through 1.5m string to make a pulling loop. Cut some streamers from crêpe/tissue paper or coloured plastic bags. Tape these to the open bottom of the bag. Decorate the bag as much as you like. Then hold the string and run, with the bag kite flying along with you. Let the wind lift it off the ground.

Sound effects

Try making the sound effects for the Bible stories. This is messy so do it outside or at bath-time! Pour some water into a flat shallow tray: this is the sea! Try blowing a path through the water. How far can you divide your sea?

Put water into a bowl and make it stormy. Swish the water with your hands, blow on it or mix it up with a hand whisk. What happens to a toy boat in the bowl?

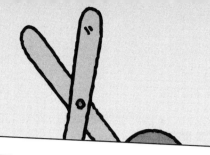

Flags and streamers

Make a flag or streamers from a coloured plastic bag and garden cane. Put the flag outside, where you can see it from the window. Check each day to see how hard the wind is blowing by looking at how much the flag is fluttering.

Adults Only

We often hear and read about 'nature' as some powerful and impersonal force but the Bible shows us that such forces (this time, the wind) are certainly not independent of God's control. Finding out about the wind will be fun for the children, but they will also be discovering an important spiritual lesson: it is perfectly possible to feel, hear, sense, see and know what the wind is doing – yet you can never see the wind itself!

Children

Brothers and sisters

How many children are there in this family? Who is the biggest in the family? Who's the smallest? How many boys? How many girls?

Can you draw yourself and your family?

What do children do?

Which can children do?
Which do only grown-ups do?

The youngest brother

1 Samuel 16:1-13

Have you got any brothers and sisters? How many? Are they older or younger than you? What do you think it would be like to have seven big brothers? That's how many brothers David had!

David was the youngest in his family; nobody took very much notice of him. His brothers were soldiers in the king's army, but David spent his time out in the fields looking after the sheep.

One day, something very exciting happened. God sent Samuel to visit David's father, Jesse. God said to Samuel, 'I've chosen one of Jesse's sons to be the new king.'

When Samuel got to David's house, his father sent for all his brothers, but not for David. Perhaps he thought David was too young and unimportant to meet someone as important as

Jesus helps a girl

Mark 5:21-24, 35-43

Jesus was busy talking to lots of people.

An unhappy dad said, 'My little girl's ill. Please help.' Jesus left the people and went with him.

Some people came from Jairus' house. 'It's too late,' they said. 'Don't bother Jesus any more.'

stories

Samuel.

Samuel looked at the eldest brother. He was tall and handsome. 'He'd make a good king; it must be him,' thought Samuel.

'Not him,' said God.

The next brother came. He was as tall and as handsome as the eldest brother.

'Not that one,' God said.

David's third brother came. He was as tall and as handsome as the eldest brother too.

'Not him either,' said God.

Jesse brought his four other grown-up sons too, but each time God said, 'No – this isn't the one I've chosen to be king.'

Samuel was puzzled. 'Have you got any more children?' he asked Jesse.

'Well, there's the youngest boy, David,' said Jesse, 'but he looks after my sheep.'

'Fetch him please,' said Samuel. When David came, Samuel looked at him. David wasn't as big as his brothers, but he was strong and handsome. Samuel liked him at once.

God said to Samuel, 'This is the one! This is the one I want to be king.'

Samuel poured a little oil on David's head, to show that one day he would be king. Even though he was the youngest in the family, God had a special job for him to do!

Jesus said, 'Don't worry. Just trust me.'

Jesus said to the little girl, 'Get up.' And she did! Jesus had made her well.

Follow up

Make a picture

Cut or tear pictures of children from magazines and catalogues. Paste them, overlapping, on to a big sheet of paper.

'When I was a child'

Ask a grandparent or an older friend about when they were children. What did they wear? What did they eat? What did they play? Have they any pictures they can show you?

A prayer

Lord Jesus, I'm so happy to know that you love me and that I'm important and special to you. Help me to remember that when something is hard or when I feel sad or frightened. Amen.

Children in other countries

Find some books about children living in another country. Talk about the differences you can see. What things are the same?

David's sheep

Make a picture of David looking after his sheep. You could paste on cotton wool (or sheep's wool if you can find some) to make the sheep. Paste on brown and green pieces to make the hills and fields. Make David from pieces of paper or fabric. Ask someone to write under the picture: 'Children are important to God.'

Concertina dolls

Make a family of children! Ask a grown up to fold and cut out some children for you to colour. Make each one different.

I am special to Jesus

Find a photo of yourself. Paste it on to a piece of card and ask a grown up to write underneath: 'My name is... I am special to Jesus. He knows all about me.'

Another Bible Story
Matthew 18:1-6

Who Is The Greatest?

Jesus' friends were arguing. 'I'm more important than you,' one said.

'You are not,' said another. 'I'm much more important than anyone else!'

Jesus heard them arguing. He called a little child to come and sit with him. He said to his friends, 'Don't argue about being important. Instead think about children like this one. You don't think they're important, but I do. Make sure they always feel loved and welcomed. Every child is special to me.'

Adults only

In a socitey that considered children unimportant, Jesus made a special point of welcoming them. He made their openness and trust an example for adults. It's good for children to grow up knowing that they matter, not only to their own family, but in their church and community too. How does your church and community show children that they really count?

Washing

Dirty!?

Can you help tell the story?

Our washing machine

Help! Our washing machine has broken down.
Whatever can we do?

We can take our dirty clothes to the laundrette.

We can scrub them in the sink as many people do.

We can wash them in a river and dry them on a bush - on a sunny day.

Or we can ask someone to mend the machine!

Which would you do?

A wash for Namaan

2 Kings 5:1-15

Naaman was a very important person and a brave soldier, but he had a secret. His skin was so sore and itchy that he tried to keep it hidden under his clothes. But somebody knew his secret, and she told him how he could be made better.

She said, 'In a faraway country there is a man called Elisha. He can ask God to make you better.'

So Naaman went to the faraway country and sent Elisha a message: 'Please help me.'

The messenger came back and said, 'Elisha says you should go and wash yourself seven times in the river.'

Naaman was very annoyed that Elisha didn't come to tell him himself. He said 'What a cheek! Doesn't he know I'm a very important person?'

Then Naaman thought, 'I've travelled so far, I might as well go and wash in the river before I go home, just to see what happens'. So he went to the river.

He waded in to where the water was quite deep.

Under the water he bobbed, then up he came.

Under the water he bobbed, then up he came.

Under the water he bobbed, then up he came.

He did that four more times. Then what do you think he saw?

His skin was clean and smooth. It wasn't sore and itchy any more! He was better!

Naaman went to show Elisha and told him, 'God has made me better!' Because he was a soldier, Naaman saluted Elisha, but the one he really said 'thank you' to was God.

Washed by Jesus

John 13:1-17

In a hot and dusty country, walking all the day,
Jesus' friends felt hot and sticky and their feet were grey.
Jesus brought some water to wash their dusty feet –
A basin full of fresh, cool, sparkling water – such a treat!

Peter cried, 'Oh no, Lord, please don't do this to me.
You're much too good to wash our feet – I'm sure we all agree.'
But Jesus said, 'I've come to be your servant to the end.
If you don't let me wash your feet I cannot be your friend.'

So Peter cried, 'Then wash me all – my feet, my hands, my head.'
But Jesus said, 'You've had a bath – clean feet is all you need.
This is what I came for – to show you what to do.
Be kind to one another, then I'll know you love me, too.'

Picture game

Which of these things would you hang on a washing line?

This is the way we wash

You can sing this song to the tune 'Mulberry bush':

This is the way we wash our hands,
Wash our hands, wash our hands.
This is the way we wash our hands
Early in the morning.

Make up other verses about washing, like 'This is the way we wash our face, feet, hair or clothes.'

Washing up

After a meal wash the plates, cutlery and cups together. Enjoy making them clean and shiny!

A soap hunt

Have a look in the shops. How many different kinds of soap can you find? What colour soap do you have in your bathroom?

Wash your clothes

Let a grown-up help you choose a few clothes to wash. Then wash them, rinse them, squeeze and wring them. Can you hang them up to dry?

Bathing the baby

If you know someone with a new baby, ask if you can watch him or her having a bath. See how careful you have to be. Perhaps you could sprinkle oil or talcum powder on the baby.

25

A picture game

How many ways of keeping things clean can you see in this picture?

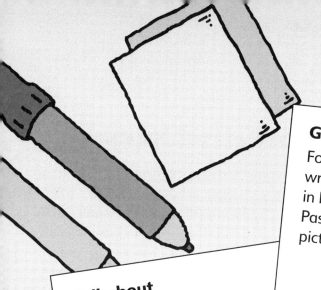

Give a present

For someone's birthday, wrap a bar of ordinary soap in brightly coloured paper. Paste a label on to it with a picture you have drawn.

Talkabout

Why is it important to keep things clean? Discuss what would happen if your skin, food or house got dirty.

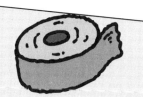

Adults only

Washing! We do it more than once every day. The Bible uses this simple action as a picture of God's desire to clean away from our lives all that is wrong and harmful. You may like to introduce this truth to your child at the right moment, but this topic aims to help everyone appreciate again the pleasure of washing and being clean again.

A patchwork prayer

Cut out pictures from magazines showing things that look clean and ways of making things clean. Paste them on to a sheet of paper and stick it on your wall. Look at this and then say a prayer:

Thank you, God, for hair that smells sweet,
Hands that are clean, food safe to eat,
For fresh beds and clothing and everything good,
For loving and caring, thank you, God.

Sun, moon and stars

Grandpa paints a picture

When Emily goes to stay with her grandpa they paint pictures together! Today they are outside painting the sun.

Grandpa says, 'The sun is beautiful – big and round and golden. But look, Emily, the sunshine has made Tess warm and sleepy.'

'I'm warm too!' Emily laughs. 'The sun warms the earth too and helps things to grow, doesn't it?'

'Yes,' said Grandpa. 'Sunshine helps all plants grow, even when it's hiding behind the clouds.

Emily added, 'I'm going to draw them as well because the sunshine helps them grow.'

Emily and her grandpa are
looking at the sky at night.
What shape is the moon?
Did you know it is
sometimes round?

Twinkle, twinkle, little star,
How I wonder what you are,
Up above the earth so high,
Like a diamond in the sky.

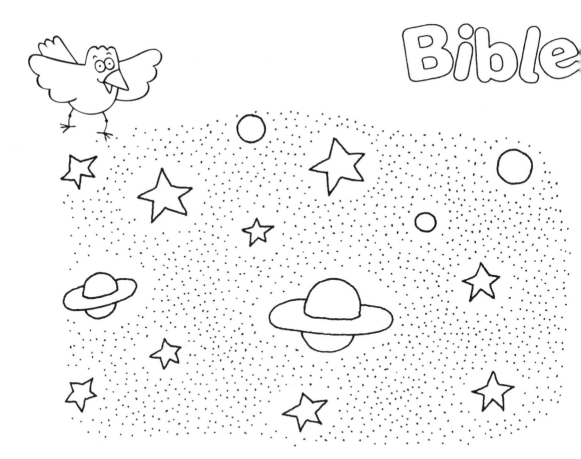

God makes the light

Genesis 1:14-19

Many years ago, long before you were born, the world was a dark, empty place. 'What shall I do?' God wondered. He wanted to make beautiful things, but that was no good if no one could see them!

So he said, 'I'll make the sun to light up the day and the moon to light up the night.' So he did. He loved the warm, golden light of the sun and the cool, silver light of the moon.

'But I'll make something else, just for fun,' said God. He made all the stars we can see in the sky, and lots more too far away for us to see – big ones and little ones, all shining brightly. There were stars everywhere in the sky. Some were close together and made star patterns.

Look at the sky one night and see if you can see the different patterns the stars make. See how beautiful they are and say 'thank you' to God.

A new star

Matthew 2:1-12

Before Jesus was born, there were some wise men in a faraway country. They saw a new star in the sky one night. It told them that a very special baby was coming to live in the world – a baby king. They said, 'Let's go and find the baby and worship him.'

'Because he is a baby king we must take him some presents,' the wise men said. So they choose beautiful presents: gold, frankincense and myrrh – just right for a special baby king. They got everything ready, climbed on to their camels and looked for the star. There it was, the biggest, brightest star in the sky. 'That's the one!' they said, and off they trotted.

They travelled for days and days and days. Wherever the star went, they would go. But one night the star stopped above a house. They went inside, and there was Jesus! They worshipped him, knelt down and gave him their beautiful presents.

At last, the wise men went on their long journey home, but they always remembered Jesus, that very special baby, and said 'thank you' to God for letting them see him.

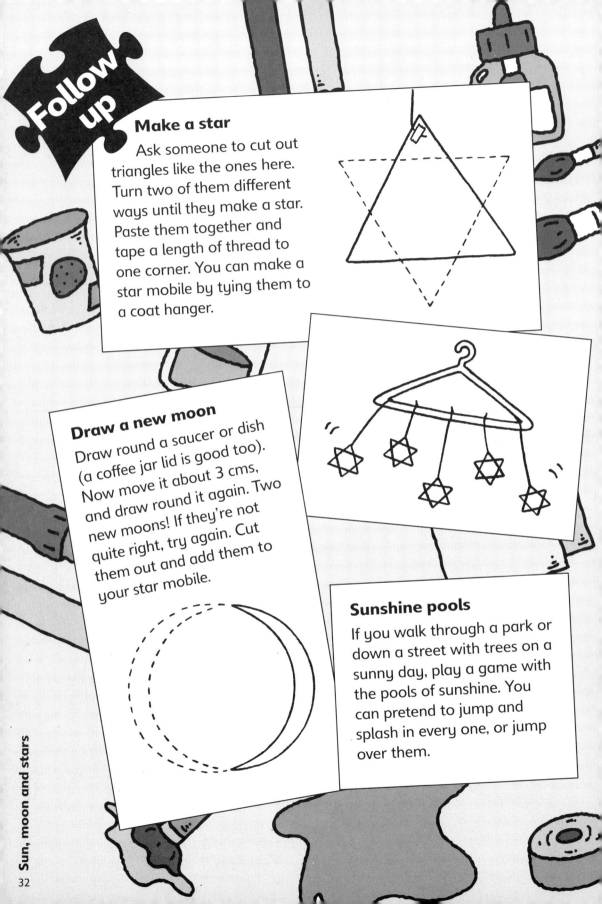

Follow up

Make a star

Ask someone to cut out triangles like the ones here. Turn two of them different ways until they make a star. Paste them together and tape a length of thread to one corner. You can make a star mobile by tying them to a coat hanger.

Draw a new moon

Draw round a saucer or dish (a coffee jar lid is good too). Now move it about 3 cms, and draw round it again. Two new moons! If they're not quite right, try again. Cut them out and add them to your star mobile.

Sunshine pools

If you walk through a park or down a street with trees on a sunny day, play a game with the pools of sunshine. You can pretend to jump and splash in every one, or jump over them.

Sun, moon and stars

Light for growing things

Grow some seeds such as cress or alfalfa. Plant them in separate dishes, water them and put one in sunlight and one in a dark place. (You will have to wait patiently for a few days!) Which do you think the plants like best?

Shadow watching

On a sunny day, go out in the morning, at midday and in the afternoon and look at your shadow. What happens to it throughout the day?

Make your own light show

When the sun is shining on a wall, hold your hand up and see what shadow shapes you can make. Move your fingers around and see if you can make an animal with ears!

In a dark room, try shining a torch to make shadows. You could use your toys to make shadows, too.

A sun, moon and star hunt

How many sun, moon and star shapes can you find? Look at flowers, leaves, fruit, wallpaper patterns and dresses and shirts. Look in your home, your books and in the shops.

Sun, moon and stars

Based on Psalm 8:3-5

Some of the Bible people wrote about sun, moon and stars. Read what they thought about when they looked at the sky.

When I look at the sky I can see how great God is. He made the sun to light up the day, and the moon and stars to light up the night. He's greater than all the world! And I'm so small. Why does he care about me?

Based on Psalm 136:7-9

God is so good! He made the sun to light up the day and the moon and stars to light up the night. Thank you, God. And thank you for loving us.

What do you think about when you look at the sky?

A prayer

Thank you, God, for the beautiful things you give us. Thank you for the sun, the moon and the stars. And thank you giving us for your son, Jesus. We need never be afraid of the dark because Jesus is always close to us. He loves us and keeps us safe, even when the skies are dark. Amen.

Good things to eat

Use a round cutter to cut out sun, moon or star shapes of pastry and bake them. (For the moon, use the cutter the way explained for drawing a new moon.) Or, if you have some very thin slices of bread, you can make sun and moon sandwiches.

Thank you, God

Sing this traditional prayer, with an extra new verse:

Thank you for the world so sweet,
Thank you for the food we eat,
Thank you for the birds that sing,
Thank you, God, for everything.

Thank you for the sun so bright,
For the moon and stars at night,
Thank you for the light they bring,
Thank you, God, for everything.
Amen.

Adults only

Sun, moon and stars can sometimes move us to wonder, as we realise the greatness of God who made everything. Do use this topic to communicate that sense of wonder to your child. It will be remembered for a life-time if you take time to be awed together!

Eyes

Where's my hamster?

Peter has lost his hamster.
Use your eyes to look at
the picture. Can you help
him find it?

What are they?

I use them when I cry,
I use them when I blink,
I use them when I see,
I use them when I wink,
And when I fall asleep,
They close.

Two blind men

Matthew 9:27-31

Jesus was very busy, visiting people, talking with them and making many people better. Lots of people followed him to see the things he did, but there were two men who could not see Jesus. They could not use their eyes. They were blind. They could not use their eyes to look at Jesus, they could not use their eyes to look at colours and they could not use their eyes to look at people.

One day, the two blind men began following Jesus. They had heard that Jesus could make people better. They could not see, but they had heard that Jesus was kind and helpful and they hoped he might make their eyes better. They wanted to see!

'Jesus!' they cried. 'Help us and be kind to us.'

Even when Jesus went into a friend's house to eat, the two blind men followed him inside.

'Jesus!' they cried. 'Help us and be kind to us.' Jesus looked at the two blind men. He looked at their eyes and knew they could not see.

'Do you think I can help you to see? asked Jesus.

'Yes, of course,' said the two blind men.

'Then let it happen just as you think it will,' said Jesus, and he touched their blind eyes.

The two men blinked. Then they blinked again, twice. Then they blinked again and again and again. They rubbed their eyes and began to look all around at the people standing watching them.

'We can see!' shouted the men. 'We can see!'

The men were very excited. Jesus had made them better just as they wanted him to. They could use their eyes to look at Jesus; they could use their eyes to look at colours; they could use their eyes to look at people. Jesus had been very kind to them after all. They could see.

Thomas and Jesus

John 20:24-29

Thomas was very puzzled. He thought Jesus was dead, but his friends were telling him that Jesus was alive, and alive forever.

stories

'How can he be alive again?' he told his friends. 'I saw that he was dead with my own eyes. How can he be alive?'

'Well, he is alive,' his friends told him. 'We saw Jesus ourselves with our own eyes and we talked with him too. You've got to believe us. Jesus is alive again!'

So Thomas was very puzzled indeed. How could Jesus be alive again? His friends must have been lying to him.

Thomas became very angry.

'Unless I see Jesus for myself with my own two eyes, I will not believe you,' he told his friends.

Then Thomas sat in the corner and sulked. He was very cross with his friends for telling lies. He heard his friends talking about Jesus. They were very excited. Thomas thought they would soon get bored with their silly game. But his friends didn't seem to care that Thomas didn't believe them. For a whole week they kept on talking about Jesus.

At the end of the week, Thomas was with his friends for a meal. His friends were still talking about Jesus when Thomas got a surprise. He opened his eyes wide so that he could see better! Someone was standing in the middle of the room and looking at Thomas. It was Jesus! He was alive! Just as his friends said! Thomas didn't know what to say, but he suddenly realised that Jesus was very special indeed.

'My Lord and my God!' he said.

'Do you believe I'm alive just because you have seen me with your own eyes?' Jesus asked. 'Those who believe I'm alive and don't see me will be even happier.'

Thomas no longer thought his friends were silly. He was really happy to know that Jesus was alive after all. He had seen Jesus, his friend, with his own eyes.

Blind man's buff

Play this game with friends. Close your eyes and spin round once. Then try to catch a friend and see who they are by feeling them. Can you guess who they are just by touching or do you have to peek?

Seeing clearly

Use a magnifying glass, binoculars or even a telescope to see the world clearly. Do things seem bigger? If you have none of these, look through magazines or newspapers for pictures of things which help people see better like mirrors, lights, spectacles, sunglasses and telescopes.

Seeing with our hands

Place different objects on to a tray and ask friends to close their eyes to 'see' what the objects are by just feeling them.

Following Jesus

Help the two blind men follow Jesus to the house where he stayed. Use your eyes and count how many houses he passes on the way.

41

The nonsense body

1 Corinthians 12:12-26

Paul wrote to his friends in Corinth.

'Just imagine,' he wrote, 'that all our body became mixed up. If we became only an eye, how would we hear? And if we became only an ear, how could we smell?

'Just imagine, 'Paul wrote, 'If our feet and hands and ears and eyes behaved so strangely.'

What a very funny body that would be!

I-spy game

Play 'I-spy' with colours. Begin by saying, 'I spy with my little eye something the colour of...' Everyone else has to guess which object has been chosen, using the colour stated as a guide.

Spectacles and sunglasses

Next time you are shopping, try to find a shop or stall which sells spectacles. Or, you might find a place which sells sunglasses to protect our eyes in bright light.

In the dark

Have you ever been in the dark and not able to use your eyes properly to see where you were going? Talk about where you were when this happened. Who was with you? What did you do so that you could see again?

Eye colours

What colour eyes do you have? Find out what colour eyes your friends and family have. How many have brown eyes? How many have green eyes, blue eyes or grey eyes?

A prayer

Dear Jesus, thank you for giving us eyes to see. Help those of us who cannot see well. Most of all, help us to remember that whether we see with our eyes or not, you are our special friend who cares for us. Amen.

Adults Only

The idea of Jesus restoring sight in the Bible is often connected with the need to believe and trust some things which we haven't yet seen with our own eyes. The fact that Jesus restored sight physically helps us to see that Jesus will also restore our faith and trust in him if we ask him to help us. We are sometimes faced with things which we can't understand, but can trust God to know what he is doing. By experiencing and enjoying in practical ways the sight they have now, your child is taking first steps in understanding something of what faith is.

Gates

Gates

Gates come in all colours,
Black, blue, white or green.
Gates keep people out
And gates let people in!

Wooden gates and
          iron gates,
Gates you can see through,
Little gates and
          heavy gates,
Gates that leave no view.

Stair gates, garden gates,
Gates in parks and schools,
Gates that lift to let
          cars through,
Gates into swimming pools.

Gates that you can
          climb on,
Gates that just get stuck,
Gates that never open
And gates that never shut.

Gates that you can
          swing on,
Gates that drag on
          the ground,
Gates that open with a key
Or shut with a
          clanging sound.

Gates come in all sizes,
Tall, wide, small or thin,
Gates keep people out
And gates let people in.

Find the pairs

Who's going to use which gate?

Josh the shepherd

A story based on John 10:7-10.

Josh is a shepherd, he has lots of sheep. Every day he takes the sheep out to the fields.

Every night Josh brings the sheep back. 'Come on,' he calls, 'in you go to the fold for the night.'

Look, the sheep are safely inside, but can you see a gate?

Josh sits across the gateway and settles down. Josh is like the gate, keeping the sheep safely inside all through the night.

Jesus said that he wants to be like Josh, keeping us safe all the time.

New gates for Jerusalem

Nehemiah 3:1-32

Nehemiah jumped out of bed. He had a busy day ahead. He had come back to Jerusalem because God wanted to rebuild the wall around the city. Once Jerusalem, a big city, had had walls around it to keep God's people safe inside. Along the walls there had been gates for people to go in and out. But now the walls and gates were all broken. Nehemiah was going to start work today to build them up again.

Lots of people helped. Nehemiah walked along the wall telling everyone what to do. 'Right, Eliashib. You and your friends rebuild the Sheep Gate. You're doing well.'

Further on, he met Zaccur and some men from Jericho. 'Great,' Nehemiah said, 'this bit of wall is nearly finished!'

He went on to the Fish Gate. 'Well done Hassenaah. You and your family have almost built this gate. Keep going!'

Nehemiah came up to Joiada. 'Where is the wood?' asked Joiada.

'I'll get you some', Nehemiah promised, 'and some more bricks.'

'Thanks,' said Joiada.

It took a long time to mend the gates and wall. Nehemiah kept walking up and down to see how it was going. He took wood to some people, bricks to others. He was very busy. Many people helped. Nehemiah couldn't count them all. Everyone did their best because Jerusalem was a special city and the people knew God wanted it to be as good as new. They worked hard together and the wall and the gates were soon rebuilt. They were so pleased when it was done, they had a party to celebrate!

A swing gate

Make a gate that opens. You will need some card from a cereal box. Draw the gate so that the bottom of the card is the bottom of the gate, cut along one side of the front and the top. Then fold down the other side. The gate should open and then shut!

Let's build

Could you build a city wall with gates from either wooden bricks or *Lego*? Perhaps all your family could help like in Nehemiah's story. You could make the houses and shops inside the city from old cereal boxes and cartons.

A prayer

Dear Lord Jesus, thank you that gates help keep us safe within our own town. Thank you that you also keep us safe and watch over us when we go out and when we come in.

Gate stories

Look at the pictures of gates on page 45. Talk about which one you like best. Say what you think is behind the gate. What would happen if you went through it?

Counting gates

When you next go for a walk see what colour gates you pass. You could count all the white gates, and all the green gates. See if you can find a big ornate gate and a little gate.

Cut and paste

Have a look through some old magazines to find a picture of a house. Cut it out and paste it on a larger piece of paper, then draw a path and a gate for your house and colour it in.

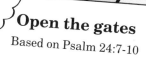

Open the gates

Based on Psalm 24:7-10

Sometimes we feel very excited and happy when we think about how great God is and all he has done for us. One of the psalmists felt like this. He talked about gates being lifted up to let God, the glorious King, come in. Here is a picture of this. What would you draw to show how great God is?

Standing inside the gates

Based on Psalm 122

I have joy, joy, joy
To be in God's special place,
Standing inside the gates.

I know love, love, love
In God's special place,
Standing inside the gates.

I feel peace, peace, peace
In God's special place,
Standing inside the gates.

Adults only

Gates are ordinary objects which we pass every day without noticing them. But in the Bible gates are significant, sometimes as a picture of our safety with God as in Psalm 122, sometimes as a picture of opening our lives to God as in Psalm 24. The topic will help your family to be more aware of gates around you and will help everyone to think about the security that God wants us all to have by knowing and trusting him.

Houses

Whose house is it?

Can you guess who lives in each house?

Moving house

Today Kerry's family are moving to a new house. How do you think Kerry feels?

All the furniture and toys from the old house are packed into the big removal van. Kerry goes in the car to the new house. It's sad saying good-bye.

Kerry's new house has a big garden, and over the road there's a park with a playground!

Moving house wasn't so bad after all! Kerry has made friends with the children next door.

The party that nobody came to

Luke 14:15-24

Do you like parties? It's fun going to parties, and it's fun when you have a party at your house. Just suppose you sent invitations and got everything ready for a party – balloons, games, music, lovely food, a parcel for 'Pass the parcel', a special cake – and then nobody came to your party! How would you feel? What would you do?

Jesus told a story about something like that.

Once upon a time, a man wanted to give a really big party. He got everything ready. There was so much food – it was a real feast! When everything was ready for the big party, the man went out to invite people. 'Come to my house for the best party there ever was!' he said. 'Everything's ready.'

But nobody wanted to come! They all made excuses.

One said, 'I'm sorry – I've just bought a field and I want to go and see it.'

Another said, 'I've just bought ten cows and I need to go and see what they are like.'

Another said, 'I'm sorry, I can't come to the party. I've just got married!'

Oh dear, no one coming to the party, with the house and the food all ready. How do you think the man felt? The man was upset, but then he had a good idea.

'I know what to do!' he said. 'I'll ask all the people who aren't usually invited to parties. I'll invite poor people, and people who can't walk, people who can't see and people nobody likes very much.'

He went out out into the streets. 'Come to the best party ever,' he told them all. 'I want my house to be full!'

stories

Jesus goes to Zacchaeus' house

Luke 19:1-6

Jesus often went to people's houses, but he met Zacchaeus in a very funny place! Zacchaeus had heard about Jesus and wanted to see him, but when Jesus came to the town where Zacchaeus lived, everyone else wanted to see Jesus too.

Zacchaeus wasn't very tall, and he knew that he wouldn't be able to see Jesus, so he ran ahead, and climbed into a tree. Now he had a wonderful view of everything! He saw Jesus coming along the road.

Jesus stopped right under the tree, looked up and said, 'Come down, Zacchaeus. I want to come to your house today.'

Zacchaeus was so excited that he nearly tumbled out of the tree. Jesus wanted to come to his house!

When Jesus came to Zacchaeus' house, he talked to him. Zacchaeus realised that he had done lots of bad things. He told Jesus he was sorry and that he would put things right. From that day, Zacchaeus was a friend of Jesus.

I'm thinking of a house

You could play this game on a journey. Someone thinks of a house you all know – perhaps granny's house, or a holiday house – and says, 'I'm thinking of a house.' Everyone else takes it in turns to ask questions, but you may only answer 'yes' or 'no'. See who guesses first which house you are thinking about.

Animal houses

Some animals make houses for themselves and some pet animals live in special houses. How many can you think of? Some of them have special names.

Houses in other countries

Look for books with pictures of houses in other countries. Some of them are very different from your own. Talk about the houses in the pictures together. Which do you like best?

Little house

All sorts of things are made in the shapes of houses like tea-cosies, candles, money-boxes and teapots. Next time you go to the shops, see how many you can spot.

A man who couldn't walk

Mark 2:1-12

Can you help tell the story? Every time you see  say 'the man who couldn't walk'. Every time you see 🧍 say 'the man Jesus made well'.

Once upon a time, there was 🛏️ He just had to lie on his stretcher all day. He was very sad, but he had four good friends. They'd heard about Jesus and decided to take 🛏️ to see him.

They picked 🛏️ and carried him to the house where Jesus was. Oh dear, the house was full of people. The friends couldn't get near the door or the windows. Then they saw the stairs up to the roof and had a good idea.

They went up the stairs, carrying 🛏️ They started to make a big hole in the roof! Very carefully, they let 🛏️ down in front of Jesus. He made 🛏️ better!

🧍 jumped up, rolled up his bed and ran back to his own house. He was very happy!

Make a Bible times house

Use the picture below of a house in Bible times. Then find a shoebox and make a house like it. If you can't manage scissors to cut out doors and windows, paste on pieces of coloured paper instead. If you have small toy people, you could use them to act out the story of Zacchaeus or the man who couldn't walk.

Build a house

If you have building bricks or *Duplo*, why not build a house? What rooms will you make?

A card house

Make a big card cut into the shape of a house. On the front, draw the roof, a front door and some windows. Then open the card and draw or paste inside pictures of furniture for all the different rooms – the bedrooms, the bathroom, the kitchen and any other rooms you'd like to have in your house. A grown-up could write, 'Thank you, God, for our house.'

Look at houses

Next time you go for a walk, take a really good look at the houses you pass. See how different they are. What are they made of? How many chimneys? What colour is the front door? How many windows? Do you know who lives there?

My house

Say the rhyme and make up some actions to go with it

I'm going to build a little house with a chimney tall,
A sloping roof and a garden wall,
A big front door you can open wide,
And two tiny windows you can peep inside.
I'm going to make a table big enough for two,
With two little chairs – one for me, one for you.
Ring at the doorbell and please come in
My little house is shining like a bright new pin.

A prayer

Lord Jesus, thank you for our house. Please bless it and all the people who live here or visit us. Help us to remember that you are always here with us too. Amen.

Adults only

This topic is an opportunity to think about the houses in which we live. Because they are so familiar, we can easily forget that they are God's provision for one of our most basic needs – shelter. As you help your child appreciate what houses are for, it will be natural to thank God for them and for what they mean in terms of safety and shelter.

Crowds

The football match

Dad is going to a football match. He is on his own.

He meets a group of friends.

Can you count them?

They join a long queue to get into the ground.

Can you count all those people?

Inside, there is a large crowd of people. There are far too many to count!

Can you find Dad in the crowd?

What a crowd!

Here is a large crowd, but nobody looks just the same as anyone else.

Point to:

the women with curly hair;

the boys wearing scarves;

the girls wearing hats;

the men who have beards.

Can you find these people in the crowd?

Who touched my clothes?

Mark 5:24-34

There was a large crowd of people around Jesus. They jostled and pushed one another to try to get near him. Some people accidentally bumped into him.

In the crowd, there was a woman who had been ill for a long time. She thought that if she could only touch Jesus, she would be made well. So, she worked her way through the crowd until she was near him.

The woman touched Jesus' cloak. At once she could feel that she had been made well. She was very pleased and turned to go home. But then she heard Jesus say, 'Who touched my clothes?'

Jesus' helpers said to him, 'Lots of people in the crowd keep bumping into you.'

Jesus knew that someone had touched him for a special reason. He knew that someone had been made well again.

He looked around to see who it was. Then the woman felt frightened because she thought Jesus might be cross, but she owned up. 'I touched you,' she said and she told Jesus about her illness.

Jesus said to her, 'Don't worry. You believed that I could help you, and I have. Now go home, and enjoy being well.'

How happy the woman was! She had a big smile on her face as she pushed her way back through the crowd and set off for home.

Crowds at Pentecost

Acts 2:1-13

There were crowds of people in the city of Jerusalem. It was festival time and many people from different countries were there.

Jesus' friends were in Jerusalem too. Jesus had gone back to God the Father in heaven, but he had promised the Holy Spirit in his place. So his friends were waiting together for him to come.

Suddenly, they heard a loud noise. It sounded like a strong wind, but it wasn't a wind. The sound filled the place where the friends were waiting. The Holy Spirit had come! The friends couldn't see a person, but they were sure he was there. It was very exciting!

Many of the people who were in Jerusalem wondered what was happening, so a large crowd gathered. There were people from lots and lots of countries – tall people, fat people, thin people, old people, young people, dark people, fair people. 'What's going on?' they asked.

So Peter stood up and spoke to them. He told them about God's Holy Spirit coming to them. The crowd listened. Some of them laughed at Peter, but others believed what he said and became followers of Jesus too.

Follow up

Potato printing

Ask a grown-up to help you print a crowd picture. First, make sure that your clothes and the table are well covered. You will need a shallow dish with some thin sponge covering the bottom. Help to mix some powder paint and put it under the sponge. A grown-up can slice a potato in half and cut out eyes, nose and mouth to make a face. You can press the potato face lightly on to the sponge (to get paint on it) and then press firmly on to some paper. Do this lots of times to make a crowd picture.

Crowd jigsaw

Cut out some pictures of people from magazines and paste them on to a piece of card. Cover as much of the card as you can, to make a crowd picture. Then ask a grown-up to cut it into 8-10 pieces to make a jigsaw puzzle.

Out and about

If you pass a school at play-time, watch the crowd of children outside. Notice that each one looks different from the others. Some are good at doing some things, some are better at other things. Every one of them is important.

Talking time

Which places do you go to where there are crowds of people? What can you see when you're in a crowd? How do you feel?

Water painting

If you have an area with paving slabs, a wall or a fence in your garden, paint a crowd of people on it with water. You only need a bowl of water and a large paint brush. When this crowd has dried away, you can paint another one!

Chalk board

If you have a blackboard, you could draw lots of faces with coloured chalks to make a crowd picture.

A prayer

Lord Jesus, we know that you often had crowds of people following you. Thank you that you loved and cared for every person in them. Thank you that you care for people who are in crowds today.

More crowds

Crowds of people often followed Jesus. They wanted to watch him helping people and to listen to the stories he told. Can you think of some times when crowds were around him? Ask a grown-up to look up some of these in the Bible: Matthew 5:1,2; Matthew 14:13-21; Mark 2:1-12; Luke 19:1-10 and John 12:12-19.

A mobile

Cut some cardboard circles 10 cm across. Draw faces on both sides of these. They can then be strung from a wire coat-hanger to make a crowd mobile.

Many people

Sing this song to the tune 'Frère Jacques':

Many people, many people,
Make a crowd, make a crowd.
Lots of men and women, lots of men and women,
Children too, children too.

Jesus loves them, Jesus loves them,
Every one, every one.
All the men and women, all the men and women,
Children too, children too.

Adults only

Jesus was in such demand during his ministry that a crowd followed him wherever he went. He had to get up early to find time to spend alone with God. Being in a crowd can be exciting, frightening or even lonely, but to Jesus a crowd was a group of individuals, each one very precious. Pray for your child as you enjoy this topic – that he or she will grow up to know that Jesus loves every single person even in the biggest crowd.